3-staff
MODERATELY ADVANCED

MW00769322

Christmas Jubilation
Carols of Joy and Peace

Jason D. Payne

Editor: Carson Cooman
Music Engraving: Lyndell Leatherman
Cover Design: Katie Hufford

ISBN: 978-0-7877-5548-5

Lorenz

A Lorenz Company • www.lorenz.com

Foreword

Christmas is a time of great joy and elation as we gather to celebrate the birth of our Savior, Jesus Christ. What better way to express this gladness than through music? *Christmas Jubilation* expresses the good news of Christ's birth through a variety of musical selections that range dynamically from a riveting "Toccata on 'God Rest Ye Merry, Gentlemen'" to a soft and tender setting of "Silent Night." Christ's birth gives us hope for a future and leaves us with happiness in our hearts as we all proclaim together, "Good tidings of comfort and joy!

Jason D. Payne

Contents

Toccata on "God Rest Ye Merry, Gentlemen"

Sw. Full
Gt. Full
Ped. Full

Jason D. Payne
Tune: **GOD REST YOU MERRY**
English Carol, 18th Century

Duration: 3:10

4

10

O Come, Little Children

Sw. Flute 8, 2
Gt. Flute 8, Doublette 2
Ped. Bourdon 16, 8

Jason D. Payne
Tune: IHR KINDERLEIN KOMMET
by **Johann A. P. Schulz**

Duration: 1:45

LL

Postlude on "Gloria"

Sw. Full to Mixtures, Reeds 8, 4
Gt. Full to Mixtures, Sw. to Gt.
Ped. 16, 8, Sw. to Ped.

Jason D. Payne
Tune: GLORIA
Traditional French Carol

Duration: 2:50

www.lorenz.com
LL

KEYBOARD

Lorenz · lillenas · soundforth · THE SACRED MUSIC PRESS

Light of the World
The Timeless Gospel Songs of Philip P. Bliss for Piano Solo
Mark Hyes

Moderately Advanced • In this volume of the Hymn Heritage Series, acclaimed arranger Mark Hayes applied his skill and harmonic genius to eight of Bliss's best-known hymns. Philip Bliss was one of the most influential songwriters in nineteenth-century America, and his sensitive, heartfelt songs continue to resonate today.

70/1982L   Piano

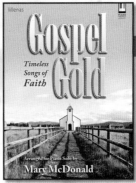

Gospel Gold
Timeless Songs of Faith
Mary McDonald

Moderately Advanced • Mary McDonald shares her enduring love of gospel songs in this creatively crafted collection of her favorites! Like the arranger herself, these arrangements overflow with boundless energy and joy that is sure to inspire pianists and grateful congregations.

978-0-7877-1495-6   Piano

The Fullness of His Love
Robert Lowry's hymns of grace and glory for piano solo
Larry Shackley

Moderately Advanced • American pastor and songwriter Robert Lowry wrote beautiful, folk-like hymns that continue to touch the hearts of worshippers. For this volume of the Hymn Heritage Series, Larry Shackley transformed eight of Lowry's classics into delightful, warm piano arrangements.

70/1985L   Piano

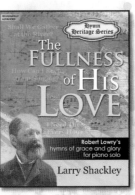

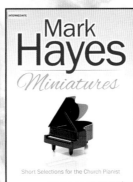

Mark Hayes Miniatures
Short Selections for the Church Pianist
Mark Hayes

Intermediate • A church pianist himself, Mark delighted in the opportunity to create this flexible collection of short, easy-to-prepare hymn arrangements and original compositions. These "bite-sized" miniatures maintain his signature sounds despite their brevity and will serve your prelude, offertory, and interlude needs during worship.

70/1940L   Piano

The King of Love
Heartfelt Hymn Settings for Solo Piano
Lloyd Larson

Intermediate • The love of God is the prevailing theme in Lloyd Larson's heartfelt collection, which offers varied styles and approaches to each hymn tune. Rich harmonies and accessible scoring allow these settings to meet the diverse needs of worship.

978-0-7877-4396-3   Piano

Beautiful Beyond Description
Classic praise and worship songs with a jazz flavor
Teresa Wilhelmi

Intermediate • Teresa Wilhelmi revisits classic songs from the early praise and worship movement, using her unique pop/jazz style to create engaging arrangements for church or home.

70/1977L   Piano

Ivory Inspirations
Creative Hymn Settings for Piano
Jay Rouse

Intermediate • As a gifted composer, arranger, and pianist, Jay Rouse's music has won its way into the hearts of performers and listeners alike for its fresh and genuine approach. These solid and creative hymn settings will appeal to pianists and worshipers of all ages.

978-0-7877-4398-7   Piano
800308145830   Performance CD

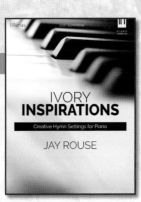

Simply Curry
Beautiful Moments of Meditation at the Piano
Craig Curry

Intermediate • Nationally known arranger Craig Curry shows his introspective side in this popular keyboard collection. The arrangements are written at an accessible level, but have all the hallmarks of Craig's creativity and skill. Ideal for quiet preludes, offertories, and communion services, the "Simply Curry" series is a resource that you will draw from again and again.

70/1647L   Vol. 1
70/1964L   Vol. 2

PIANO FOR ALL SEASONS

For complete contents, audio samples, level descriptions, and a list of our partnering dealers, look and listen at www.lorenz.com

Spirituals
For Piano Solo
Emma Lou Diemer

Intermediate • Award-winning American composer Emma Lou Diemer applies her keyboard creativity to sixteen traditional American spirituals, in a collection that will find a place in churches, schools, and recital halls.

70/2004L   Piano

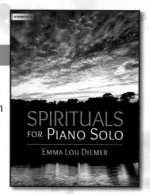

The Church Pianist's Library
Volume 20

Intermediate • Drawn from our long-running periodical *The Church Pianist,* each volume of *The Church Pianist's Library* contains 104 pages of music that is satisfying to play but technically accessible and presented in a handy wire-bound format. The music is linked to the church calendar, and each piece is timed to help you plan ahead.

70/2025L   Piano

A Time for Adoration
Inspiring Moments of Worship for Piano Solo
Sandra Eithun

Moderately Easy • Sandra Eithun has a rare talent for writing creative, musical hymn arrangements that are easy to learn and rewarding to play. *A Time for Adoration* encourages reflection on the greatness of God and His beautiful creation.

70/2019L   Piano

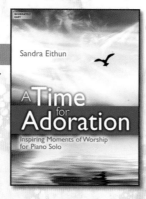

To God Alone Be Glory
A Reformation Celebration for Piano Solos
Stephen Nielson

Advanced • World-renowned keyboard artist Stephen Nielson presents a brilliant collection of hymns based on the core beliefs of the Reformation: scripture alone, faith alone, grace alone, Christ alone, to the glory of God alone. These challenging arrangements are suited for worship or recital use.

70/1980L   Piano

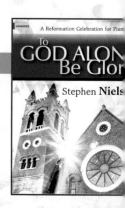

Old-Time Gospel Favorites
Golden Age American Gospel songs for piano solo
Anna Laura Page

Intermediate • Anna Laura Page has selected 10 of her favorite 19th-century American Gospel songs and given them sparkling new settings, ranging from quiet reflections to boisterous celebrations in this exciting collection.

70/2038L   Piano

In Jubilant Song
Proclamations of Faith for Solo Piano
Gina Sprunger

Moderately Advanced • This collection of well-known, traditional hymn tunes is especially suited for festive occasions throughout the church year. Gina Sprunger creates and appealing blend of arrangements full of infectious vitality and energy balanced by a handful of reflective selections.

70/1997SF   Piano

4-Hand Piano

Come, Christians, Join to Play!
Creative Hymn Settings for Piano Four-hands
Mark Hayes

Advanced • "The only thing better than playing a solo is sharing the joy with a partner on the bench." Mark Hayes said it, knows it, and Mark Hayes proves it in his second book of four-hand piano arrangements. Featuring favorite gospel songs, spirituals, and American folk hymns, this collection includes something for everyone.

70/1945L   Piano, 4-hands

The Glories of My God and King
4-Hand Settings for Piano
Molly Ijames

Intermediate • These dramatic four-hand piano arrangements feature Molly's signature rich harmonic language and creative writing style. The inspiring collection includes some of the most beloved and timeless hymns of faith—suitable for the entire church year!

978-0-7877-4394-9   Piano, 4-hands

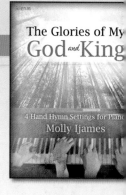

A Eugene Butler Organ Treasury
Eugene Butler

Moderately Advanced • One of America's most beloved choral composers, Eugene Butler is well known to musicians for his more than 1,000 published works. This treasury presents Butler's entire output for organ, offering a mixture of original and hymn-based compositions that explore a variety of styles and moods.

70/1973S   Organ, Three-staff

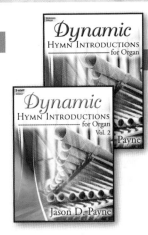

Dynamic Hymn Introductions for Organ
Jason D. Payne

Moderately Advanced • Written for use in Jason Payne's own church, these major hymn tunes received energizing introductions that are designed to uplift congregations in singing with renewed spirit and vigor. The first role of any church organist is to serve as an effective worship leader, and these gems of inspiration are guaranteed to heighten that corporate experience.

70/1822L   Vol. 1 – Organ, Three-staff
70/1970L   Vol. 2 – Organ, Three-staff

Mark Hayes: Spirituals for Organ
Artistic Expressions of Faith and Joy
Mark Hayes/arr. Marvin Gaspard

Moderately Easy • Mark Hayes's artistic expressions of faith and joy once again grace the organ rack, this time thanks to the care of Marvin Gaspard. These spiritual arrangements draw on the jazz, blues, and gospel side of Mark's writing, and the results overflow with passion and character.

70/1966L   Organ, Two-staff

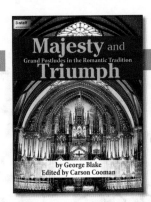

Majesty and Triumph
Grand Postludes in the Romantic Tradition
George Blake

Intermediate • George Blake's postludes provide ideal conclusions to worship services, and his music in the grand romantic tradition, possessing a distinct majesty, is among his finest. Carson Cooman edited each piece for clarity, brevity, and use on modern organs.

70/1971L   Organ, Three-staff

Go Out With Joy!
Short Postludes for All Seasons
Mary McDonald

Intermediate • In answer to many requests for shorter postlude choices, Mary McDonald crafted these splendid collections of works for Christmas, Easter, patriotic/family celebrations, Thanksgiving, and the new year. These arrangements are quick to prepare, and their thrilling sounds will set the perfect mood for the close of your services.

70/1889L   Vol. 1 – Organ, Three-staff
70/1969L   Vol. 2 – Organ, Three-staff

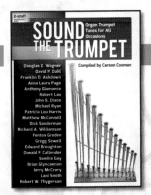

Sound the Trumpet
Organ Trumpet Tunes for All Occasions
Compiled by Carson Cooman

Moderately Easy • Including fourteen works commissioned specifically for this book, *Sound the Trumpet* offers twenty-three trumpet tunes that range from majestic and stately to thoughtful and introspective. In addition to their usefulness for postludes, preludes, and recitals, many of these pieces offer unique selections for weddings.

70/1953L   Organ, Two-staff

Organ and Piano Duets

Festive Preludes for the Church Year
Dramatic Organ & Piano Duets
Lani Smith

Intermediate • Reflecting Lani's dedication to providing church musicians with quality and practical music, this rousing collection of duets provides exciting arrangements for the most celebratory days on the church calendar. These stirring works exhibit his mastery of keyboard color and texture. Two copies are required for performance.

70/1937L   Piano and Organ, Three-staff

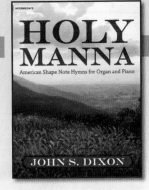

Holy Manna
American Shape Note Hymns for Organ and Piano
John S. Dixon

Intermediate • Having withstood the test of time, the early American hymns of our musical heritage have great intrinsic merit. John Dixon arranged six of these classic shape note hymns in his accessible style for organ & piano duet. All of these pieces make excellent preludes, offertories, or postludes for worship, and suites of multiple pieces can be easily assembled for a recital.

70/2018L   Piano and Organ, Three-staff

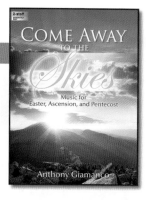

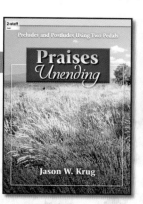

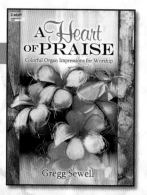

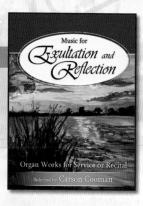

18

Silent Night

Sw. Strings 8
Gt. Soft Flute 8, Sw. to Gt.
Ch. Warm Solo
Ped. Soft 16, 8, Sw. to Ped.

Jason D. Payne
Tune: STILLE NACHT
by **Franz Xaver Grüber**

Gently, with expression ♩= ca. 80

Duration: 3:50

Variations on "I Saw Three Ships"

Gt.   Flute 4
Ped. Principals 16, 8, Flutes 16, 8, Sw. to Ped.

Jason D. Payne
Tune: I SAW THREE SHIPS
Traditional English Carol

Variation I

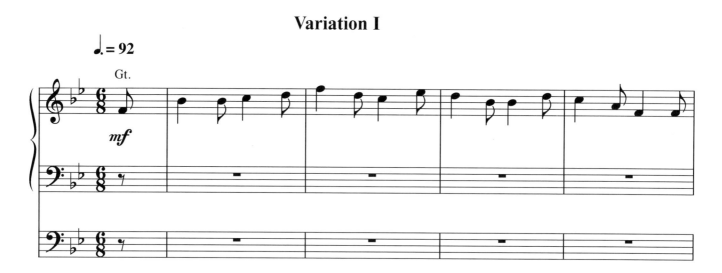

Duration: 6:00

LL

Variation II

Sw. Voix Celeste 8, Flute Celeste 8
Ch. Principal 8
Ped. Soft 16, 8, Sw. to Ped.

Variation III

Gt. Flute 8, 2
Ch. Flute 8, 2 (echo-like)

Variation IV

Sw. String Celeste 8, Flauto Dolce 8
Ch. Flute 8, 1⅓
Ped. Soft 16, 8, Sw. to Ped.

Variation V

Sw. Full
Gt. Full
Ped. Full

32